C000110381

A Cream Cracker Under the Settee

A monologue from Talking Heads

Alan Ayckbourn

A SAMUEL FRENCH ACTING EDITION

SAMUEL
FRENCH

FOUNDED 1830

SAMUELFRENCH.COM
SAMUELFRENCH-LONDON.CO.UK

A CREAM CRACKER UNDER THE SETTEE

First shown on BBC TV on 24th May, 1988. The cast was as follows:

Doris   Thora Hird
Policeman   Steven Beard

Directed by Stuart Burge
Produced by Innes Lloyd
Designed by Tony Burrough

Subsequently performed as part of the stage version of *Talking Heads*, which opened on 11th January 1996 at the Octagon Theatre, Bolton. The cast was as follows:

Doris   Ann Rye
Policeman   Rod Arthur

Directed by Lawrence Till
Designed by Martin Johns
Lighting designed by Fiona Lewry
Sound by Paul Bunn

AUTHOR'S NOTE

The set should be kept simple. There is no point in constructing an elaborate set (still less a series of sets) and just putting one person in the middle of it all. Less, in this case, is more; the simpler the setting, the more the audience is required to use its imagination and concentrate on the performer. If you want costumes and scenery do *Carousel*.

A CREAM CRACKER UNDER THE SETTEE

*The living-room and hallway of Doris's semi-detached house.
Morning*

*The living-room is suggested by a settee, an easy chair and a table
but not much more. In the corner is the door to the outside, with a
letter box. There is a cream cracker under the settee and a wedding
photograph in a broken frame lies on the floor too*

Music. The Lights come up

*Doris, in her seventies, sits awkwardly on the easy chair and rubs
her leg. She has a duster*

The music fades

Doris It's such a silly thing to have done.

Pause

I should never have tried to dust. Zulema says to me every time she
comes, 'Doris. Do not attempt to dust. The dusting is my department.
That's what the council pay me for. You are now a lady of leisure.
Your dusting days are over.' Which would be all right provided she
did dust. But Zulema doesn't dust. She half-dusts. I know when a
place isn't clean. When she's going she says, 'Doris. I don't want
to hear that you've been touching the Ewbank. The Ewbank is out
of bounds.' I said, 'I could just run round with it now and again.' She
said, 'You can't run anywhere. You're on trial here.' I said, 'What
for?' She said, 'For being on your own. For not behaving sensibly.
For not acting like a woman of seventy-five who has a pacemaker
and dizzy spells and doesn't have the sense she was born with.' I
said, 'Yes, Zulema.'

She says, 'What you don't understand, Doris, is that I am the only person that stands between you and Stafford House. I have to report on you. The Welfare say to me every time, "Well, Zulema, how is she coping? Wouldn't she be better off in Stafford House?" ' I said, 'They don't put people in Stafford House just for running round with the Ewbank.' 'No,' she says. 'They bend over backwards to keep you in your own home. But, Doris, you've got to meet them half-way. You're seventy-five. Pull your horns in. You don't have to swill the flags. You don't have to clean the bath. Let the dirt wait. It won't kill you. I'm here every week.' I was glad when she'd gone, dictating. I sat for a bit looking up at me and Wilfred on the wedding photo. And I thought, 'Well, Zulema, I bet you haven't dusted the top of that.' I used to be able to reach only I can't now. So I got the buffet and climbed up. And she hadn't. Thick with dust. Home help. Home hindrance. You're better off doing it yourself. And I was just wiping it over when, oh hell, the flaming buffet went over.

Pause

You feel such a fool. I can just hear Zulema. 'Well, Doris, I did tell you.' Only I think I'm all right. My leg's a bit numb but I've managed to get back on the chair. I'm just going to sit and come round a bit. Shakes you up, a fall.

Pause

Shan't let on I was dusting.

She shoves the duster down the side of the chair

Dusting is forbidden.

She looks down at the wedding photo on the floor

Cracked the photo. We're cracked, Wilfred.

Pause

The gate's open again. I thought it had blown shut, only now it's blown open. Bang bang bang all morning, it'll be bang bang bang all afternoon. Dogs coming in, all sorts. You see, Zulema should have closed that, only she didn't.

Pause

The sneck's loose, that's the root cause of it. It's wanted doing for years. I kept saying to Wilfred, 'When are you going to get round to that gate?' But oh no. It was always the same refrain. 'Don't worry, Mother. I've got it on my list.' I never saw no list. He had no list. I was the one with the list. He'd no system at all, Wilfred. 'When I get a minute, Doris.' Well, he's got a minute now, bless him.

Pause

Feels funny this leg. Not there.

Pause

Some leaves coming down now. I could do with trees if they didn't have leaves, going up and down the path. Zulema won't touch them. Says if I want leaves swept I've to contact the Parks Department.

I wouldn't care if they were my leaves. They're not my leaves. They're next-door's leaves. We don't have any leaves. I know that for a fact. We've only got the one little bush and it's an evergreen, so I'm certain they're not my leaves. Only other folks won't know that. They see the bush and they see the path and they think, 'Them's her leaves.' Well, they're not. I ought to put a note on the gate. 'Not my leaves.' Not my leg either, the way it feels. Gone to sleep.

Pause

I didn't even want the bush, to be quite honest. We debated it for long enough. I said, 'Dad. Is it a bush that will make a mess?' He said,

'Doris. Rest assured. This type of bush is very easy to follow,' and fetches out the catalogue. ' "This labour-saving variety is much favoured by retired people." Anyway,' he says, 'the garden is my department.' Garden! It's only the size of a table-cloth. I said, 'Given a choice, Wilfred, I'd have preferred concrete.' He said, 'Doris. Concrete has no character.' I said, 'Never mind character, Wilfred, where does hygiene come on the agenda?' With concrete you can feel easy in your mind. But no. He had to have his little garden even if it was only a bush. Well, he's got his little garden now. Only I bet that's covered in leaves. Graves, gardens, everything's to follow.

I'll make a move in a minute. See if I can't put the kettle on. Come on leg. Wake up.

Music. The Lights fade to Black-out

Doris sits on the floor with her back to the wall

The music fades. The Lights come up

Fancy, there's a cream cracker under the settee. How long has that been there? I can't think when I last had cream crackers. She's not half done this place, Zulema.

I'm going to save that cream cracker and show it her next time she starts going on about Stafford House. I'll say, 'Don't Stafford House me, lady. This cream cracker was under the settee. I've only got to send this cream cracker to the Director of Social Services and you'll be on the carpet. Same as the cream cracker. I'll be in Stafford House, Zulema, but you'll be in the Unemployment Exchange.'

I'm en route for the window only I'm not making much headway. I'll bang on it. Alert somebody. Don't know who. Don't know anybody round here now. Folks opposite, I don't know them. Used to be the Marsdens. Mr and Mrs Marsden and Yvonne, the funny daughter. There for years. Here before we were, the Marsdens. Then he died, and she died, and Yvonne went away somewhere. A home, I expect.

Smartish woman after them. Worked at Wheatley and Whiteley, had a three-quarter-length coat. Used to fetch the envelopes round for the blind. Then she went and folks started to come and go. You lose track. I don't think they're married, half of them. You see all sorts. They come in the garden and behave like animals. I find the evidence in a morning.

She picks up the photograph that has fallen from the wall

Now, Wilfred.

Pause

I can nip this leg and nothing.

Pause

Ought to have had a dog. Then it could have been barking of someone. Wilfred was always hankering after a dog. I wasn't keen. Hairs all up and down, then having to take it outside every five minutes. Wilfred said he would be prepared to undertake that responsibility. The dog would be his province. I said, 'Yes, and whose province would all the little hairs be?' I gave in in the finish, only I said it had to be on the small side. I didn't want one of them great lolloping, lamp post-smelling articles. And we never got one either. It was the growing mushrooms in the cellar saga all over again. He never got round to it. A kiddy'd've solved all that. Getting mad ideas. Like the fretwork, making toys and forts and whatnot. No end of money he was going to make. Then there was his phantom allotment. Oh, he was going to be coming home with leeks and spring cabbage and I don't know what. 'We can be self-sufficient in the vegetable department, Doris.' Never materialized. I was glad. It'd've meant muck somehow.

Hallo. Somebody coming. Salvation.

She cranes up towards the window

Young lad. Hallo. Hallo.

She begins to wave

The cheeky monkey. He's spending a penny. Hey.

She shouts

Hey. Get out. Go on. Clear off. You little demon. Would you credit it? Inside our gate. Broad daylight. The place'll stink.

A pause as she realizes what she has done

He wouldn't have known what to do anyway. Only a kiddy. The policeman comes past now and again. If I can catch him. Maybe the door's a better bet. If I can get there I can open it and wait while somebody comes past.

She starts to heave herself up

This must be what they give them them frame things for.

Music. The Lights fade

Doris sits on the floor in the hall, her back against the front door, the letter-box above her head.

The music fades. The Lights come up

This is where we had the pram. You couldn't get past for it. Proper prams then, springs and hoods. Big wheels. More like cars than prams. Not these fold-up jobs. You were proud of your pram. Wilfred spotted it in the Evening Post. I said, 'Don't let's jump the gun, Wilfred.' He said, 'At that price, Doris? This is the chance of a lifetime.'

Pause

Comes under this door like a knife. I can't reach the lock. That's part of the Zulema regime. 'Lock it and put it on the chain, Doris. You never know who comes. It may not be a bona fide caller.' It never is a bona fide caller. I never get a bona fide caller.

Couple came round last week. Braying on the door. They weren't bona fide callers, they had a Bible. I didn't go. Only they opened the letter-box and started shouting about Jesus. 'Good news,' they kept shouting. 'Good news.' They left the gate open, never mind good news. They ought to get their priorities right. They want learning that on their instruction course. Shouting about Jesus and leaving gates open. It's hypocrisy is that. It is in my book anyway. 'Love God and close all gates.'

She closes her eyes

We hear some swift steps up the path and the letter-box opens as a leaflet comes through. Swift steps away again

She opens her eyes

Hallo, hallo.

She bangs on the door behind her

Help. Help. Oh stink.

She tries to reach the leaflet

What is it? Minicabs? 'Your roof repaired'?

She gets the leaflet

'Grand carpet sale.' Carpet sales in chapels now. Else sikhs.

She looks at the place where the pram was

I wanted him called John. The midwife said he wasn't fit to be called anything and had we any newspaper? Wilfred said, 'Oh yes. She saves newspaper. She saves shoeboxes as well.' I must have fallen asleep because when I woke up she'd gone. I wanted to see to him. Wrapping him in newspaper as if he was dirty. He wasn't dirty, little thing. I don't think Wilfred minded. A kiddy. It was the same as the allotment and the fretwork. Just a craze. He said, 'We're better off, Doris. Just the two of us.' It was then he started talking about getting a dog.

If it had lived I might have had grandchildren now. Wouldn't have been in this fix. Daughters are best. They don't migrate.

Pause

I'm going to have to migrate or I'll catch my death.

She nips her other leg

This one's going numb now.

She picks up the photo

Come on, Dad. Come on, numby leg.

Music. The Lights fade to Black-out

Doris sits with her back against the settee under which she spotted the cream cracker

The music fades and the Lights come up. It is getting dark now

I've had this frock for years. A lame woman ran it up for me that lived down Tong Road. She made me a little jersey costume I used to wear with my tan court shoes. I think I've still got it somewhere. Upstairs. Put away. I've got umpteen pillowcases, some we got given when we were first married. Never used. And the blanket I knitted for the cot. All its little coats and hats.

She puts her hand down under the settee

Here's this cream cracker.

She rubs the cracker

Naught wrong with it.

She eats it

Making a lot of crumbs. Have to have a surreptitious go with the Ewbank. 'Doris. The Ewbank is out of bounds.' Out of bounds to her too, by the looks of it. A cream cracker under the settee. She wants reporting. Can't report her now. I've destroyed the evidence.

Pause

I could put another one under, they'd never know. Except they might say it was me. 'Squatting biscuits under the settee, Doris. You're not fit to be on your own. You'd be better off in Stafford House.'

Pause

We were always on our own, me and Wilfred. We weren't gregarious. We just weren't the gregarious type. He thought he was, but he wasn't. Mix. I don't want to mix. Comes to the finish and they suddenly think you want to mix. I don't want to be stuck with a lot of old lasses. And they all smell of pee. And daft half of them, banging tambourines. You go daft there, there's nowhere else for you to go but daft. Wearing somebody else's frock. They even mix up your teeth. I am H.A.P.P.Y. I am not H.A.P.P.Y. I am un-H.A.P.P.Y. Or I would be.

And Zulema says, 'You don't understand, Doris. You're not up to date. They have lockers, now. Flowerbeds. They have their hair done. They go on trips to Wharfedale.' I said, 'Yes. Smelling of pee.' She said, 'You're prejudiced, you.' I said, 'I am, where hygiene's concerned.'

When people were clean and the streets were clean and it was all clean and you could walk down the street and folks smiled and passed the time of day, I'd leave the door on the latch and go on to the end for some toffee, and when I came back Dad was home and the cloth was on and the plates out and we'd have our tea. Then we'd side the pots and I'd wash up while he read the paper and we'd eat the toffees and listen to the wireless all them years ago when we were first married and I was having the baby.

Doris and Wilfred. They don't get called Doris now. They don't get called Wilfred. Museum, names like that. That's what they're all called in Stafford House. Alice and Doris. Mabel and Gladys. Antiques. Keep them under lock and key. 'What's your name? Doris? Right. Pack your case. You belong in Stafford House.'

A home. Not me. No fear.

She closes her eyes. A pause

Policeman's voice Hallo. Hallo.

Doris opens her eyes but doesn't speak

Are you all right?

Pause

Doris No. I'm all right.
Policeman's voice Are you sure?
Doris Yes.
Policeman's voice Your light was off.

Doris I was having a nap.
Policeman's voice Sorry. Take care.

We hear the Policeman go

Doris Thank you.

She calls again

Thank you.

Long pause

You've done it now, Doris. Done it now, Wilfred.

Pause

I wish I was ready for bed. All washed and in a clean nightie and the bottle in, all sweet and crisp and clean like when I was little on Baking Night, sat in front of the fire with my long hair still.

Her eyes close and she sings a little to herself. The song, which she only half remembers, is "Alice Blue Gown"

Pause

Never mind. It's done with now, anyway.

Music. The Lights fade to Black-out

FURNITURE AND PROPERTY LIST

On stage: Settee
Easy chair. *On it*: duster for **Doris**
Table
Cream cracker
Wedding photograph in broken frame

Off stage: Leaflet (**Stage Management**)

LIGHTING PLOT

Practical fittings required: nil

Interior. The same scene throughout

To open: General interior lighting. Morning effect

Cue 1	**Doris**: "Wake up." Music *Fade to black-out*	(Page 4)
Cue 2	**Doris** sits on the floor. Music fades *Bring up lights to same setting*	(Page 4)
Cue 3	**Doris**: " ... frame things for." Music *Fade to black-out*	(Page 6)
Cue 4	**Doris** sits on the floor in the hall. Music fades *Bring up lights to same setting*	(Page 6)
Cue 5	**Doris**: " Come on, numby leg." Music *Fade lights to black-out*	(Page 8)
Cue 6	**Doris** sits against the settee. Music fades *Bring up lights to evening setting*	(Page 8)

EFFECTS PLOT

Cue 1   As play begins   (Page 1)
           Music

Cue 2   **Doris**: "Wake up."   (Page 4)
           Music

Cue 3   **Doris** sits on the floor   (Page 4)
           Fade music

Cue 4   **Doris**: "...them frame things for."   (Page 6)
           Music

Cue 5   **Doris** sits on the floor in the hall   (Page 6)
           Fade music

Cue 6   **Doris**: "Come on, numby leg."   (Page 8)
           Music

Cue 7   **Doris** sits with her back against the settee   (Page 8)
           Fade music

Cue 8   **Doris**: "It's done with, anyway."   (Page 11)
           Music

Lightning Source UK Ltd.
Milton Keynes UK
UKOC01f0328180214

226616UK00002B/3/P